The Brittle Sea
NEW AND SELECTED POEMS

for my sleeping boys –
Ioan, Jack and Joe.

Paul Henry
The Brittle Sea
NEW AND SELECTED POEMS

Seren is the book imprint of
Poetry Wales Press Ltd.
Suite 6, 4 Derwen Road, Bridgend,
Wales, CF31 1LH

www.serenbooks.com
Follow us on social media @SerenBooks

The right of Paul Henry to be identified as
the author of this work has been asserted in accordance
with the Copyright, Designs and Patents Act, 1988.

© Paul Henry.
First published 2010. Reprinted 2013 & 2023.

ISBN: 978-1-85411-524-9

A CIP record for this title is available from the British Library.

The publisher acknowledges the financial assistance of the Books Council of Wales.

Cover painting: 'Poet Crossing' by Anthony Goble.

Printed in Bembo by Severn, Gloucester.

Author's website/blog: www.paulhenrywales.co.uk

Contents

from *The Milk Thief* (1998)

from *The Slipped Leash* (2002)

Round the corner is – sooner or later – the sea.

Louis MacNeice – 'Round the Corner'

from *Time Pieces* (1991)

Widows of Talyllyn

They lived as needed, hid their strength,
survived the male, modestly,

block the aisle on the market bus,
still see husbands in summer fields,

still wear rings on mortal fingers,
grasp cupfuls of chipped memories,

wake at sober dawns and leave
their precious days unsquandered.

Fire Builders, Llangynidr

And the green country, should I turn again there?
My bumpkin neighbours loom even ghostlier: ...
                    Robert Graves – *On Dwelling*

I

Harder to see them, half-wood
half-boy, shambling about
over the vague roots,
seeming to know where each piece goes.

Flagons jut from rock pools,
suspiciously, periscopes up.
Stahl's cheap tape recorder
sings as if through a snorkel.

A snap under Sharky's boot.
Smoke foul-hooks a flame or two,
enough to fetch the bottles
surfacing like prize fish.

They are kissing the glass lips
of absent village girls, cursing
their mothers for keeping them in,
inhaling their private fires.

How long have they been there?
Prosser lugs a mighty slab
nearer the embers, lets out a cry.
It closes like a door on the light.

II

Sharky's barn burns inside: the boys
are slugging Bow, seeing Bill off again.

His eyes fit to burst, mouth gagged
by the bottle's heavily knuckled rim.

He flexes his handshake arm, each swig
enlarged on the corrugations behind him.

*

They imagine Australia, Prosser and Joe
inside the long lane home, sheep coughing

deep in the hedges, a Friesian smouldering
through a gate – lines of latitude, bars

over a map of the world. Bill's gone.
Infinity waits around the next bend.

*

The dark sock of the lane is tipping
them out towards a lamplight at the end.

III

A schizoid sky above the A40.
Rainbows, rare cocktails
pour into limpid hills.

I want the god-given crayons,
to colour in the perfect
beginning, middle and end.

And then it darkens, unreal,
rubber spools in slow motion
breaking hard to a halt.

Clean out of miles they come at me –
Prosser, Stahl, big-handed,
the rest of the boys, leaping large.

Men now, from lane to lane
straying across the borders
of grey, adult behaviour.

I put my foot down, go to them
over hard acres of silence,
expecting nothing:

                        a handshake,
a look that stirs
a rainbow swimming in oil

a fire in the rain perhaps.

Cwm Dyffryn

for Glyn 'Sharky' Price

Respectable now, my pale hands
direct the hoover's plough,
ejecting from the carpet
the crumbs between its furrows.

Its drone becomes a tractor's,
fifty miles, ten years away,
gritting its teeth in the earth,
unlocking them shining.

You had sentenced me to stones,
to wade in each new wound
spurting red in your wake
and clear its clotted throat.

One hour stretched me out
on the rack of my spine
to my limit and I snapped,
dug deep in the soil

for an unstitched pocket
embroidered with worms,
hooked you from your element
with worms, your biggest fear.

The Massey Ferguson rolled on
into the dark without you.
Only the late birds caught
our laughter in that valley.

Respectable now, my pale hands
unplug such incidents,
the characters of dust
ascending in a silent room.

Syd Bowen

More chapel than public house
though still village property,
one they'd call their own.

There were less and less like him,
dark-suited old boys
who took on the hedges by hand –

Griff Price, Vernon Probert,
Tommy Farmer – squeezed out
by the press of generations.

I name trees after them.
Their summers hung about us
in our sense of not belonging.

Syd Bowen's here I think,
though last I saw of the man
he grew towards me, smiled

passed the time of year,
shrank again, was gone ...
into the privacy of lanes.

The Village, A State of Untruth

The village, a state of untruth,
a blunt tongue in a butcher's shop,
the warp in a time-scrubbed block.
You have come back to what never was.
For *Please Drive Carefully*, read
Enter At Your Own Risk.
The churchyard understudies the pub.
The stone wall of the school divides them.
Like wool on a thorn, its name
clings, like unwanted love.
A stranglehold on its youth
lies broken in each grave.
There is no clock, only a stream,
an overhead cheese-wire's hum.
And perhaps you are dreaming this.
Would it not have been safer
to preserve it for suburban friends
on a wall, or in that sheep's skull
next to the fruit on the sideboard?
The village's collective mind
has settled in the lull
between question and answer.
Its memory is long.
It haunts, like the heart
cut for the butcher's son
still there on the old yew,
or the map of blood
that clung to his apron
the summer he almost broke free.

Honeymoon at Castletownsend

You stand in the east-wing window,
framed in its twenty-four panes,
his lovely red template
over a view of the bay,
its own babe in arms
after the storm last night,
swishing back and fore
its curtains unhooking,
hushing itself to be calm.

Love's accidental symmetry
is broken as he notices
a cracked pane to your left,
a hint of varicose vein
on the back of a sunlit calf,
a wasp hanging by its life
in a web just outside
like one of the tassels
above the four-poster,
sprat-like, swimming
the seam of its shoal
on the heater's warm air.

You brush out the night,
the tangled past from your hair,
casting out his doubts beyond
the frayed hem of a shoreline
sighing over its rings.

Buried Treasure

Three silver shells, two feathers,
twisted into a black net,
placed in a young sailor's palm,
small interpreters of love.
He falls backwards into sand.
Nothing so profound as this
has happened so easily, so far.
'You keep me safe,' she says.

Continents later discover him
an older man, a dull cabin.
He has been at sea too long.
On turning the key of a small box
he is faintly surprised
to find the contents still shining.

Busker

Chagall's black-eyed violinist
is busking outside Saint David's Hall,
blue-handing Irish jigs to the air,
to the mad hats of a serious town, gulls
in a shabby perfection of flight
above the Hayes Island snack bar.
The tune shivering on is the one
another fiddler used to play
and I bow down to the open case
in the manner of taking, not giving,
of placing an ear to a cold stone
and catching the tail end
of a river that went underground.
Taken for granted in full spill
somewhere steeply greener than here.

It surfaces now, snatches at feet
and fills an empty pocket of time
with a currency of belonging.
As out of his hands again, the wild
ignited flock
will not stop dancing overhead

will not stop dancing, minutes after
the slim shadow man,
in search of another precinct,
slackens and slips out of sight.

Saline Helen

A silver stem in the grey
and all your unspecified summers flower,
come back to me now on Mynydd Llangorse.
As if, so many years in advance
you had planned this visit, impatient
on Traeth Gwyn for a cloud to break,
for the sea to reach our bare feet,
time to run out from between our toes.

You've surfaced, my Salacia, again
saline, up the slope to *Penllain*.
Today you swam with a dolphin.
An old woman shoos you in.
Already the holiday moves inland.
Your red towel hangs in state
on the yard's gently fading tan

while down on the hardening sand
the fisherboys set their dividers,
turn and throw the sun a lifeline,
reel in curses out of the dark.

Clouds drag their nets to the hills
where I wait for you on this sodden track.
Jump on my shadow if you like.
Or leave me holding this stalk of light.

———

from *Captive Audience* (1996)

Double Act

It's only a passing hum,
the waste collection.
We leave before it's come

or after it's gone,
or precisely at the time
the sacks are taken away

or not at all; calm,
breathless, holding out
the ghost of a note

in each other's arms –
Ray and Renie Gray:
Children's Magicians,

Distance No Object.
Speciality:
Birthday Parties.

Still pulling albinos
out of love's top hat,
still up to the act.

A tortured dove crows
under a purple sheet.
Look. Or go blindfold.

The King and Queen of Hearts,
still not too old
for the dark arts.

Down time's sleeve,
fallen … fallen …
onto this huge bed.

A flick of the wrist
and now you see us
suddenly white-haired –

Ray and Renie Gray:
Distance No Object.
Keeping the van and the phone,

holding on to that smile,
the *Yellow Pages* ad,
avoiding the pot-holes

along the night road,
for fear of vanishing
into them.

★

After the flaccid wand,
the silent gun,
the naughty kiddies,

after the last light-switch
of the last, echoing hall
of the last function

a warm hand,
Ray and Renie, two halves
of the same soul,

a wave, a flurry, a kiss
and this ... and this ...
and this ...

Conditioning

Our avant-garde family unit tilted
its buggy into Old Compton Street,
and before you could say 'Boy, Boy, Boy'
I was in your brother's salon, *Rox*,
letting his hands, dead replicas
of your father's, cleave 'disastrous' hair.
Quicker than words, they worked in *Lamaur's*
'Hi Gleam'. You cried laughing

and I wondered who had shaved his hair
so close to the skull, and how often,
and if the stunned, peroxide strands
were his way of holding time in place.

*

At the other extreme of the motorway,
that night, in your father's butcher's shop,
in the passage way, I watched him scrub
another bloody silence from his hands,
then bless the sleeping baby's locks,
then scrape a finely-ribbed curl
of congealed, fat-like coconut-oil
from the sloughy depth of a small jar

and then, with the same blunt hands,
in front of the same cubit of mirror,
rub the carcass beyond trace,
work the gel invisible.

Unfinished Work

The Town Planner's labyrinthine dream
observes, from the aquiline heights of his sick-bed,
a sunlit field of rape rising towards him,
smothering whole the crumpled map in his head.

Visitors, at the times allotted, do not
park their cars directly outside his house
but a metre or so to the left or to the right.
The permutations of their routes suffice
as entertainment.

                              These three, too politely
on cue, he has reworm, from *Z* to *A*,
their journey; then informs them, sedately,
how they might have come another way.

His wife bears in a tray, with three teas
and a glass of water. The neighbour's loft extension
still hangs in the balance, and it's *Yes* –
No – *Yes* to *The Castle's* flashing neon,
at this stage.

                    So long as air blows
through a window's open lip, however thin
or polluted, there will be decisions, laws
to ponder over, after the guests have gone,

when the sun's golden, uncharted terrain
slowly

                    refines him

                              out of the plan.

A634 NKX

When the old ambulance broke down
my sister's kids got out and pushed,
all nine of them, and gradually
she'd be driving towards another birth,
picking up speed, laughing
like the two-year-old in the wake
of the suddenly farted-out smoke.
She'd thank God as the engine coughed
and there was life, as a heave of labours
grew in the mirror into a stampede of souls,
more laughter in the English suburbs.

Lance, they called it, for short.
It smothered Father Patrick's weekends,
clipped the kerbs of dreams at night
when faded into abortive silence,
collected stray leaves between tyres

while under their posters of turtles, cars
and the Bessed Virgin Mary, they slept
on the smooth rides of their bunk-beds,
my sister and her nine loves,
freewheeling towards another green light.

At New Quay

Too near to the pleasure boat queue
my cousins, in low-slung deckchairs,
impersonated in turn by their girls,
are sunlit with an intensity
that plays more with some than others.
How the tides move in and out of them,
my confident, sisterly cousins - how time
keeps them skinny and brown. The future
frills at their ankles. Sails bloat
brilliantly to their half-salutes.
How naturally married they've become.

(Engraved on the front's headstone
their walk back winds then disappears
behind *The Black Lion,* then curls
up to Francis Street and opposite
the bowling green slaps its shoes
on their grandmother's step.

                                Inside
the walls flesh out, the attic bathes
in its new conversion, only the stairwell
refuses to give up its smell. The doorbell
scrunches up its note in waves
diminished by distances opened and closed.
Four generations of women pass
through the porch's stained glass
and the village barely twitches a net).

Deliberately, faintly miraculous,
they pick up their bundles and go,
my cousins, the suddenly torturous sun
alighting the spines on their arms,
their feet sinking in tired millenniums,
their bony toes instinctively holding true.

Comins Coch

Coming in from the yard, we unlearnt
the natural dance of play, stiffened
into rows, one for each class, hands
reaching to touch the shoulder in front,

to establish neat spaces. Miss Jones,
our referee, after the shuffled pack
took order, would double-check
her game of patience on the linear stones.

She once broke the cane on Emyr Brees,
set him homework to cut another
from his father's hedge. Quiet Heather's
tears ran down her knees.

On the canteen wall, Sir Ifan ap
Owen M. Edwards, above the sprouts
and the gooseberries, turned away, motes
of the alphabet caught in his sun-trap.

Time spelt us right. We got xylophones,
slide-rules, projector screens,
trips to Chester Zoo and St Fagans,
a topic on Ghana's coffee beans.

Miss Jones started to smile. The smell
of swede from the kitchen grew tame.
I pulled on the ring of the steel frame
so the field hung at an angle

in the huge window all afternoon,
waiting for the bell. We discussed,
in English: Carlo, George Best
and the next Apollo. The blackboard spun.

With her back to us, that last Friday,
with her bucket, her housecoat over her dress,
she might have been polishing glass,
not square, chalk-marked infinities.

For X and Y

God love the zimmer-frame,
the Social Worker's absorbent smile,
the hand-rail, detachable limb,
smoke-alarm, peep-hole,
the nest egg, the ancient fruit
still caught by Titan's chariot
in X and Y's maisonette,
the spats and the flimsy white hat.

God love their sallow babies
tucked away in a cradled bag,
the melanotic leaf on a bough
about to snap, the oblique wig,
bread and wine on wheels, the prayer,
the Dental Technician's pride, the crust,
the limpet-like corn plaster,
the seaside town Chiropodist.

God love the adapted plug,
the bath tub's elevating chair,
the cure for heartburn, the box of figs
unopened since 1964,
the sleeping pills, the rack of pipes,
the one tot of sherry, the lie.
God love the flutter, the papers,
the reading glass and the new sky.

God love the Daycare Nurse,
the old songs, the incontinent tales,
the monologues and the listeners,
the rain that brings out the snails.
God love the hearing aid –
THE HEARING AID! – the view of the bay,
their shells and their sugary blood,
their stitches in time, their silver days.

And God love the wedding they wore,
that hangs in a blind must

                              that waits
for a hand on the difficult door
and then

                  for a chime of light.

Love Birds

They rendezvous each night, at ten,
for ten minutes, behind closed eyes,
he in his cell, she in the brown rocker.
And once a fortnight, for half an hour,
their fingers form a desperate nest,
remembering the robin he'd fed
that misses him at the back door,
its freedom disorientated.

The screws must laugh at these love birds,
each week's confetti of letters,
or secretly gain faith from matching
her sentences to his.

He hears her singing *Porgi Amor*
in the difficult, unreal dawns
when the walls barge further into him
and terrible lights flash in his mind.
When the bars of his hands close tightly on
what might prove the last breath
of some precious, invisible creature.

She knows all this, waiting
in the early kitchen, lovingly timing
two cracked eggs in a saucepan.

Fighting It

The white-coated acupuncturist
picks up an arm's twig, its scarred
open palm drooping, holds the wrist
and closes her eyes to the figure on the bed

or, more professionally, couch.
So there is time to notice the fat Buddha
on the mantelpiece, his belly's pouch
full of calm, to absorb a passing car

to sense two cultures harmlessly collide.
Her forehead is a temple to her age.
On its dome the day's light begins to fade.
I watch its frown slowly disengage.

The ceiling's world, a sallow map of damp,
looms over flesh plastered in needles.
It might, it might not fall, all is limp
under the sterilized spines, more or less.

Charts on a wall display the body's meridians
from lateral, post- and anterior view,
a join-up-the-dots man or woman
showing where the pins go into you.

She listens, out of an intense whiteness,
a moment, before extracting the latent heat,
as if an overlong summer had caused distress
to a child removing last flowers. I wait

outside her clenched eyes again. It is all
a question of belief – in icons, nature,
her shoulder-length hair playing waterfalls
with love, somewhere else warmer, not here.

At This Hour

A neighbour ventures out to paint his gate.
Cars open and close the acts of dreams.
The cleansing properties of the estate
get to work, begin to seep at the seams.

Arms and feet slip through the bars of their cots.
A sigh lets love go at last.
Ties forget themselves, out of their knots.
Someone else's egg is forecast.

Another black hole waits to be starred.
You turn on your side and the bed slides to the wall.
The soul of a house groans behind its facade.
Moon-struck roofers rehearse how to fall.

The Sorting Office factory-farms the mail.
Sealed eyes read up on how to cry.
Glazed marriages hang by a single nail.
The paint on the brilliant gate starts to dry.

Bunk-beds

I love their deathly poses –
Marat and Chatterton,
their soft chains of roses
easily kicked down,

their arms dangled at 5 a.m.,
their torsos arced in mid swim,
their heads tilted for dreams.
No technology touches them.

Perfectly unsprung faces
inform the past
on what the future releases.
Time unclenches its fist.

At the first hint of light
I kiss them good night.

Daylight Robbery

Silent as cut hair falling
and elevated by cushions
in the barber's rotating chair
this seven-year-old begins to see
a different boy in the mirror,
glances up, suspiciously,
like a painter checking for symmetry.
The scissors round a bend
behind a blushing ear.

And when the crime's done,
when the sun lies in its ashes,
a new child rises
out of the blond, unswept curls,
the suddenly serious chair
that last year was a roundabout.

All the way back to the car
a stranger picks himself out
in a glass-veiled identity parade.

Turning a corner
his hand slips from mine
like a final, forgotten strand
snipped from its lock.

The Unsung Park

Sunday morning. We younger men
come to fight for a watery egg,
to drift spasmodically between
the gates of Heaven and Hell.

My touch-judge on the edge of speech
studies a red leaf as it falls.
It dives for the line. He picks it up,
waves it like a warning flag.

A blue day unravels its gauze.
Heavily hung-over trees applaud
the face pressed to the wet grass.

Small worshipper, take my shirt.
We are both of us playing for time.
Your mother crosses herself on the path.
Growing too old for this game, I am
breathless as winter branches,
cursing all my missed conversions.
Soon it is only a question of who
will perceive (on catching the cold sun
through my bones) the scrawl of an empty nest

eggs flown between the uprights.

The Breath of Sleeping Boys

Something is about to happen.

Legs are crossed fingers.

A cup falls from its handle.
A wall crumbles into the road
under the weight of a flower bed.

In their dreams
something is about to happen.

Saved and damned, saved and damned –
the breath of sleeping boys.

One wave breaks, another inhales
and something is about to happen.

Shrubbery trembles, blatantly.

November the 5th in Lilliput Road.
The introvert is out of its lid,
reads and repeats the word BANG

until the tarmac sky translates
madness back into stars, a life
into mute, mouse-like slippers.

Something is about to happen. *Sh.*

Here is the sound (let it pass)
of young blades, wading through grass.

The town's terrarium anticipates
that something is about to happen.

The wind adjusts its volume.

Peace carries a wicker basket.
Her dress takes in the new breeze.

With each step she's moving out,
stork on her heels, almost in flight.

Something is about to happen.

Winged eyes in a blameless dark
beat inside their hemispheres.
Their lashes are feathers dipped in oil.

Deeper than ocean beds, their dreams
rebuild Atlantis in domed air.

Saved and damned, saved and damned –
the breath of sleeping boys.

Brothers

A kick, the dance of a can in time.
They drop lines off a bridge, luckless,
fight over headstones, draw blood
to preserve a name bandaged in moss.

Gate-crashers, another dream
gives them house-room, thin ghosts
playing cards under a tin lid.
They clench their grins and pebbly fists.

Or again, soft-hoofing it down a lane
belch into laughter as one falls,
impales his hand on a black thorn,
smiles at the sudden rose that fills

the gift of his outstretched palm.

Fatherless Friends

Like untopped ferns they grew absurdly tall,
swayed on touchlines while others chased a ball

crossed their legs and frowned ahead of their time.
To one, theft was the only natural crime.

Now he builds homes while another interprets dreams
and a third dissects pianos in empty rooms.

Odd reunions bring their gentle beards
towering over my boyish smile, their cords

worn at the knees and, almost fatherly,
their massive, priestly hands, protecting me.

The Voice

A voice, after closing-time,
is singing outside the prison wall,
within earshot of the cells,
a voice from another country,
singing without knowing,
a voice in the habit of crazy acts
and familiar with buckets of water.

A voice that might have been a voice,
it sings across the brittle night,
after the inquests of dreams begin,
suddenly dropping, like glass onto stone,
from a high note to a low one.

Tears become luminous at its feet
before, protesting, it moves on.

House

Something keeps this drainpipe
clinging to the wall,
these rags to their line,
this roof to the felt interior.

It might be the boys
racing snails
in the back yard, or the sun

casting you in your past,
or this holiday,
or the first ice-cream van

or the last, or the breeze
plucking the blinds,
humming inside a sound-box.

I watch the pegged out marriages
grow and retract,
grow and retract,

love's deep-breathing exercise
in time with the wind.

*

A blue curtain
by an open window
is the summer's concierge.

It carries your love
up to an airier room,
where Rodin's *Clouds,*

the sole exhibit,
moves you to sighs.
(In a dark annexe

the moon jangles its stars.)
Holding on to the frame
I watch you fly,

the trees rejecting
countless drafts
and ending up with sky.

*

The snow has built
a village out of the town.
Strangers pick up words

mould them again,
pelt each other
with persiflage.

The face on the glass runs.
Under the giant quilt
there's talk of peace,

two cold noses kiss,
cars are dumbfounded,
neutralized.

All two feet are
equal except for
the sizes of their shoes.

*

Look down from your silence,
your fine, Roman nose.
Here, in an unmade garden

the dead have floated
up to their branches
and back into their buds.

Hold your breath.
Something now.
Habitually.

Spring.

from *The Milk Thief* (1998)

I
Aber

Winnie's

I slide an arm into the cool
between sofa and cushion

                        the pool
where the razor-shell waits

                     find
what naturally swims to hand –

the sprung spectacle case she forgot
and

         priceless when opened out
to the sun

              his dappled frames

with her lenses inside them.

Replica of a Sunshine Home for Blind Babies, Aberystwyth

Did no one take a brick to this glass case?
　　A ball and chain?
Now I'm old enough to press my face
　　to the brittle pane

without their ghostly hugs around my gaze
　　it comes home –
how time's a shell of the snail it was,
　　a smaller room.

What miniature, sunken eyes remain look out
　　from a pantheon
that keeps this town's unstable light,
　　as I look in,

trying to read the Braille of the years between,
　　with no clear sign
but, conjured back and fore by the sun,
　　their faces in mine.

The Hourglass

Ghosts of the architects move in.
Down town the moon floats
across Great Darkgate Street.

The hour gained finds my father
teasing the wheel through his hands
as if he'd invented time,

as if we could rise in his Bubble
up to the stars' infinite tides
and drift back home.

He breaks south of the pier
that creaks and leans out too far
on its zimmer-frame, points

to the same joke. *By God!*
It's Auntie Dwyn! (Victory
on her column) *Still there.*

Cue my sister's Petula Clark,
her tiny womb's pod
already bursting into song.

★

The singer swallows eggs raw
and talks all day in whispers
before a recital, draws

a pebble-headed crowd.
It's her house of sighs,
her love that skews

like a gull between clouds,
that harbours lullabies.
When I clap she always bows.

★

The King's Hall and the Waun chapel
are still singing.

Sing in their heads.

Bethesda and Tabernacle.

Sing in their heads.
Sing in their heads.

Seilo and the castle choir.
Sing. Sing. Sing.

Tros y Garreg
Mynwent Eglwys

Dafydd y Garreg...
Ar Hyd y Nos

Sing. Sing.

Y Deryn Pur
Y Gwcw Fach

Y Ferch o'r Scer
Gwŷr Harlech...

Sing in their heads,
their grey, spectacled heads.

★

The sixties undress.
Flowers lay crumpled and strewn
in heaps along the coast.

My father looks down
from the salty rail,
his bald patch turning brown.

★

Wil T. and I

squint through slats
on hands and knees,
avoid the sperm whale spits

of the rising tide.
The gipsy's wink,
once mechanized,

dooms us to DRINK
TOO MUCH AND DIE.
(Her theatrical tank

dispenses cards
that smell of ash.)
We can't afford

a second wish.
Between the boards
our futures flash.

Just before they hit
the rocks they fly.

*

The giant paper bellows
sigh, page after page,
shaken back to shape like pillows.

I put it down to age.

*

Ann Walters, town soprano,
waving her daughter off
down intricate lines

remembers to give
one last tip, her shout
more of a recitative

as the train pulls out.
Julia!
Don't forget!

Packet soooooooooooup!

Slowly, bar by bar,
her back to the engine,
my sister forgives her.

★

They chime through the dark
like perfectly struck tuning forks,

walk out without keys
under the unswept stars.

Old needles clatter onto the lawn.
His treeful of *I.O.U.'s* holds on.

The moon diminished, at daylight
the first notes take flight.

The piano between them has aired
the spirit of unloved wood.

She waits nervously in her gown.
Nobody counts her in.

She opens her mouth to sing
and the silence is deafening.

★

Sprawled out on murderous carpets
I play with the same toys –
the unicycling clown, the snow-dome,
the bear with insomniac eyes ...

or pick up *Gulliver's Travels*
still eared at page 1,
oblivious to all but the music
until the quiet draws in

and I drift about in search of them –
the voice and the violin –
wander into dust-showered rooms
as if after something stolen,

panic to find in the furniture
their misplaced harmonies.
Tears scale down the stairs.
I watch the waterline rise ...

wake up tethered
where stone looks shine
on the bay's draining board

and washed up lines
I'd fish for at first light
are weighted, snagged, entwined

about the rocks' lie,
where the hour's glass, caught
in pools, momentarily,

sees them walk, side
by side, my sighing family,
into the oncoming tide.

Calcutta Sandals

Thirty years after the war and still
your sluggish toes would emerge
for summer, indecently.

The struggle
to slip the small, braided noose
over the big one embarrassed me.

Flesh and chappal curled at the edges.

And yet they smelt fatherly,
like your Bombay watchstrap,
gave credence to your sermons.

After shoreline forays,
you'd slap their soles together
like a self-applauding seal

then put them out
to dry on the back step

until the warm air finally cooled
on those long, August evenings
and, like all your other "dog-ends" –

the tiny elephants (unpacked
half their original size)

your tin trunk's moth-eaten dhoti

the untouchable hookah –

they came apart in your hands.

Waunfawr

My mother's coffee morning crew,
their wrinkled smiles turned cold,
their haloes rinsed blue

are not so much old
as suddenly wrecked by love
in a strange town. Only the gold

on the rim of an ear's cove,
a cup's tilted ring
or a mast-like crucifix was saved.

I remember the bright billowing
of their sails on the balcony,
that caught the wind blowing

twenty years too late. Now the sea
sips away at her tired crew
and empty china stares back at me.

Welsh Incident

In the early hours of September 3rd, 1997, a giant
turtle was found dead, on the shoreline at Cricieth.

The *Cambrian News* reporter's car
blocks the lane down to the shore.

Someone plays the bagpipes
where the last field meets the sea.

But for the randomness of the tide
she'd still be gracing the waters
of a century as it drowned.

Armour-plated, run aground,
a creaturely grief mourns her end.

Two elderly, village paparazzi
circle the wreckage, take snaps
before the oceanographers descend.

Holiday Home

This house, built on clay, the last
to slide into the sea,
splits its sides with parting cracks
by those who signed the book:

the Burns of Slough, 1959 –
This Shangri-La of Wales must never die!...

Dunkirk's very own
Dot & Ken, June '65 –
Flymo broken. Shears first class!...

and, lest we forget, *Rex The P-o-ET!*
whose pawprint authenticates
some doggerel from 1972.

The Burns return in '86, retired,
smug, children's professions listed
as if it counted: Accountant, G.P.,
Lawyer and ... one missing
from *Our Infamous Four!*

Thirty-nine summers

assembled and folded away
neatly, into a fractured box,
like jigsaws, cards or dominoes

lined up purely to be felled
by the tide, which raises the stakes
with each turned over wave.

Here's the owner, Spring '98:
Hilary B – *Down for repairs,
to keep this place afloat!...*

I take in her skewed watercolours
and books, half-comforted
that someone still flies with Biggles,
pedals, bare-kneed, to Smuggler's Top
up the stairwell's 1 in 1.

Sunday Englishman, I sleep
almost imperially
on these suspect foundations,

happy to dream the same dream
as those who signed its sheets
without thinking, with love,

whose breakages, like mine,
are paid for by the sea's refrain –

Come back … come back … come back …

II
The Visitors

The Visitors

The women of my earliest years
fill this room's empty bay
without warning –

                    Brown Helen,
Catrin Sands, Gwyneth Blue,
Nightingale Ann ...

                    Their songs
return to a stranger's hand
the keys to all past tenancies,

Heulwen, Dwynwen, Bron Y Llan ...

I lie back, let them haunt,
the soft pulse of their lips
against the stone wall I've become,

Heather, Geta, Prydwen Jane ...

listen hard across the dark
as their voices fade again,

Edith Smart, St Julia ...

sleep with the bedroom door ajar
in case they should drift back in.

Brown Helen

Floats on a cushion
in the parlour at *Penllain*.
The sun through frayed nets
drowns the smell of must.
A plankton of dust
swims in the space between us.

I saw you. Don't look down.
You picked it,
then you rolled it
then you flicked it.
I saw you!

Were she not so brown
and terrifyingly thin
and certain a witness

I might have surfaced sooner
without salt in my eyes.

Catrin Sands

Ready about ... lee-oh!

Cabin-boy to her Bligh
I need to hook a bass
then cook it for her sandy hair.

Instead, it's sea sickness
I catch, and blue, blue air.

Gwyneth Blue

Locked in the lifeboat shed
with Nightingale Ann.

What if no one had come –
not the tide, nor the sun

nor love,
nor love's Harbour Master, birth?

And what if the gun
out on the horizon
had never sounded?

She emerges into the light,
shielding her laughter.

Following swiftly after
her petticoat's wake

the handsome blue boat
slides out

on its way to save.

Nightingale Ann

She'd raise one brow
like the circumflex over the o in môr.

or that curved bough
arching the Dwyfor,
her River Lachrymose.

I laid my poacher's lines at her feet
and traced a tear's course
from cheek to lip, then tasted it.

She told me the history of her rings,
the vocabulary of birdsong.

"Look away" she said
and, fool, I did,

turning back to a half-dressed tree
her blue eyes poured into,
a sudden shoal of leaves at my feet

and, on the stone where she sat,
a small circle of salt.

Heulwen

Still holding on to the sea rail
I taste and imagine another life
that's slippery with the salt of her bones.

Too much whiskylight.

Get back to that dark house,
its tea and antiquity,
its po and shotgun under the bed,

its attic clouds

conveying the summer's regattas elsewhere.

So I lie one more night
by the old oak screen
with candles and eyebright,

lie one more night
in the flowerlight
with heather and celandine,

lie one more night
by the old oak screen

with sand in my hair
and salt in my dreams –
craving another *dead dear.*

Dwynwen

Her pearl necklace snaps
in the Coliseum, spills
its countless ways.

           A crab
between the shushing aisles
I glance up to the light
and see

          Dwynwen's bride,
deaf as a silent movie,
hurling flowers at small girls.

I can't find her pearls,
am drowning in feet

and now she wants to join me
down here –

          the loudest whisper
in the universe, her accent
perfectly preserved

belonging to the child
who, to *The End,*

must live out her dreams underwater.

Bron Y Llan

Of the sharp words and the blackberry tarts
and the poultice that drew out the black thorn
from this hand

              which warms her wagging scorn
in a fountain pen –

             her suddenly bleeding heart.

Heather

Forgive me this apple I stole
some thirty years ago

when your hair was brown, and mine
as fair as this four-year-old's

who offers it back to you now
sweet Heather, hauntingly.

Is it summer or autumn?
The years collect on the lawn.

You show us the latest extension
to the house time almost didn't see.

Then you start to cry as, guiltily,
I lift my shadow up to your tree.

Geta

She's a fine white yacht
a cool airy distance away.

Make space for her, make space.

Make space and you will notice
she's drifting nearer the shore.

Make space, make space.

You have waited long enough
for this love to harbour.

Prydwen Jane

Even more mystified once
right now she'd settle for mad,
at eighty outliving me to shame –
Africa, Egypt, the Philippines ...
but she wants more "time, time, time ..."
and shakes her fist at God
along the quiet lane to Cei Bach.

She repeats the latest: Prydwen, in transit,
from Florida to Gatwick,
the only nurse on a doctorless plane,
instructing the pilot whether to land
in Atlanta or go "on, on, on ..."
at the casual flick of her hand.
Though here, in the quiet lane to Cei Bach,

she shudders inside my donkey-jacket,
fragile, angry still
from the sight of Gwyneth Blue's grave,
as we pass by the unbleating loves,
glimpse the bay's shimmering lull,
"witness, witness, witness, witness..." the sunset
ending the quiet lane to Cei Bach.

Edith Smart

Diving into her blue dress
she leaves another creaking board,
admits the awkward fit of her age
then rises to break the surface

of another day, *Edith Beatrice
Walters* – swimmer, talker, pianist,
playing a till's dissonant keys,
cleaving the ham, turning its page

across a counter's glass bay,
abusing the gift, seizing the joints,
drowning home at six to play
Mendelssohn's *Songs Without Words*.

St Julia

Dancing to Motown in her room
with Brown Helen and Catrin Sands.
She might be teaching me how to swim –
first the breast-stroke, with hands
that open and drift like seaweed
into reverse, now the suntanned
front crawl ... Their skirts wind
like mermaids' tails in the gloom.
The scales fall away.

          There's barely time
to realign white headbands
between tracks, to suddenly become
The Supremes, to apportion blame
for wrong steps, to further dim
the lights

      to mime a scream

III
Newport East

Newport East

The booths close in two hours.
Ice-cream vans are on overtime.
Twinkle-twinkle ... Arthur Scargill's
voice passes down the hill.
The only true Socialist candidate ...
is addressing the slow sunset,
fathoms deeper by the word.
The town's coral gathers about them,
the sun and Arthur Scargill,
going down together,
one gracefully, one burning still.

The Glebelands

Boats, like fallen window-boxes
sink in the mud, bloom with weeds.

Bulbous-headed kids on the bank
manoeuvre first bikes like drunks.

Soon they'll perform tricks
in streets named after Romantics.

Alf sniffs at a chained gate
where Sam inhales Bill's shit.

The art school's lime cupola runs,
hangs in a Turneresque haze.

The river pedals after the sun.
The paint flakes off the trees.

Draped in gold, like tired gods,
men surface from the underpass.

The Park Girls

Belch like toads at closing time
and pitch their laughter in keys
sopranos dream about.

The wind pushes their empty swings,
the rusty cogs and pendulums
of a clock beyond repair.

Round and round the park they go,
disturbing the inertia of a town
that turns anti-clockwise

about their screams.
Small crimes confess themselves
between the barbed railings –

a hairgrip pinches a condom's
stocking top, a needle
lurks in the buttercups.

In the searchlights of a car
they balance on heels, arms out
like novice tight-rope walkers.

Even the rain can't tame them.
They shelter inside the arms
of a yew and start to sing.

Inside the *MIND* Shop

The fake snow-spray's giant kiss
in the mirror's *Merry Xmas*
marks the spot that wills to fit
the giant into the midget.

A finger skates on the counter's pane
where a baby's boot waits to be claimed,
where Ritchie, phone tucked under his chin,
might be playing the violin
or conducting *Silent Night,*

where records, shoes, books and ties
are memorials to the Seventies,
where there's time to contemplate
the third world stuff – rugs, cushions,
a carved bird, skull caps ....

A club-foot kicks a box of cups.
Mary glances down from her wig,
hugs her faded *Woman's Own*
with its haloed baby on the front.
Something of everyone is wanted.

On rails, the dead drip at the cuffs
with tags, beyond bar-codes,
absorb the rain brought in,
a charmed sprig of incense.

A mitten picks up a snow dome
and shakes another storm
for the figurine children on their farm
who've seen it all before.

The door's cowbell does not distract
the white-bearded browser.
He stares himself out in the mirror,
clears his throat and, suitcase in tow,
tries another *Ho! Ho! Ho!*

Through Green Railings

Prints in the long-jump sand,
a woman's feet and hands.

The space between take off and land,
what was it? The distance between

the earth and the moon,
the first kiss and the honeymoon?

All those years in flight.
I cling to the railings' measured light

and think I catch her shadow flit
in a gull's.

                For a second's breeze
the missed trajectories

of her love and mine synchronize,
hold hands in mid air

turn to smile at each other
on the leap's highest tower

and kiss ...

                before the ecstatic climb

lets go

                falls back down out of time.

Hey Diddle-diddle

Here's only the eloquence of sleep
finding its tongue, the last sheep
hurdling the cemetery stone,
the bleat of abandoned head-phones,

only the knives and forks talking,
the dogs and spoons barking.
A soft-shoe-shuffle disappears
into smooth, arched ears.

Falsetto boughs break.
The tom in the moon aches
to hear their lullabies, makes a wish.
The years turn cold in his dish.

The wind bows a pylon's *A*.
Small dreams are still at play.
Starved quadrupeds on the plain
ignore the passing train.

from *The Slipped Leash* (2002)

The Short Cut to the Sea

No one's charted this way
except by heart. The bay
opens up at the end.

Already stitching the torn land
back to the dazzling sea
or bending to untie
the straps from your brown feet,
you've left me behind.

Wait for me! Wait!
cries the land to the sea.

Acts

There are months of not loving you
when the plates we keep spinning
simply spin – but today I woke
and broken china surrounded the bed
and nothing rhymed.

                          I limped
into a small garden and wept.
The grass washed my poor feet.
Through the shed's cracked pane
some dust made a merry-go-round.

Today was loving you again

and knowing that, outside of grief,
the plots of soaps drone on,
the commentaries from transistors
on allotments, the bees in the fuchsias,
the trains slowing down or gathering speed
with somebody on them thanking Christ
they don't live here, or there ...

I have given up trying to piece together
so many broken plates, to perfect
the circus acts of love.

                          I remember
that once upon a rippling field
the sun's big top came to our village,
its bright mast stretching out
like a path to the horizon,
how the sand slipped from under our feet
and the sea left its staves in our hearts.

I remember that much of loving you.

★

One shirt, one dress on a line
(such acrobatics – the leaves hold their breath
and then applaud) yours and mine –
the closest we'll come to a fall.

★

How is the knife thrower?
Of all the eyes in the audience
he picked out yours. And so it was that,
after he'd made you his squaw,
I watched you turn weak at the knees

and somewhere, beneath all the smiles,
heard the lions roar.

★

There are months of not loving you
when the lion tamer's charm is enough.
She's easily as brown as you
and the jungle in her eyes
matches the ocean in yours.

But when she leaves the cage ajar
an impulse makes for your shore.

★

Today the strongman cracked.
The tributaries in his neck
erupted with lava.
His fixed grin crumbled
and an avalanche of teeth
bit the dust.

When he fell
the whole house shook and the weights
spun off the end of all he'd held dear.

Glancing in the mirror he saw
Saturn without its rings,
Christ without his halo,
the Mona Lisa without her smile,
a universe of ash ....

★

There are months of not loving you,
empty domes for the mildly insane,
where The Prozac Clowns rehearse ...
Timing, timing is everything!
calls Zac to Coco (on his arse
with a blade through his brain).

And there are days, tumbling days
that steal your thunder,
when the woman spinning by her smile
could be anyone.

But not this day.
I missed you in the lunch-hour crowd,
the pull and push of its currents
beneath my aching feet

and every so often,
through tears in the canopy,
your blue eyes staring back
from another time.

Giant Leaps

What chapel lives we might have had!
What parsimonious slices of love!
With Salem over the upright
and *Crist yw pen y tŷ hwn* ...
and the century cornered inside our *Bush*.
Its organ-stop buttons alternate
between *Dechrau Canu* ... and Apollo 11.
Look! There's Neil (you be Neil)
and here's me, Buzz, upstaged
but glad to be still in the race.
We smack the sofa's arms
and watch the stardust rise,
stress no more than a sermon
to polish when the Lay's away.
What chapel lives! One small step
surely, with such a simple set.
Warm your palm awhile my dear
on this faithless cabinet
and pray for our time as it dies.
Beyond your window's crucifix
Newton, Einstein, Edison
and other village luminaries
walk their curious frowns
as far as the lane's end.
Small incinerations of thought
rise between the birdsong as they pass.
The graveyard's crooked equations
and pipeman's philosophies
wait, patiently, for a solution.
Don't stare at the sun too long dear.
Take off this prickly shawl.
Ours the black book and kettle,
the standard lamp in the hall,
the blues under the pews
and the laptop under the bed.
What chapel lives we might have led!

A Model Railway

Peering in through windows we see them,
our parents, dimly lit
"for authenticity", reading *Wizard*
or *Girl's Own* ... or buying another hotel
on Old Kent Road, speculating
for dreams, between the tracks
and broccoli-like trees.

Or are they the ones in the tunnel,
whose hair he painted white,
who wait in darkness for a signal,
remembering the war?

                    A whistle blows.
On a platform, holding their pose,
Trevor Howard and Celia Johnson
won't let go, won't let go.

The Slipped Leash

It sways from a branch out the back
and from it hangs a nut cage.

The handstrap still whiffs of him
for all the wind and rain –
sea dog, country dog.

What misfits we'd have made,
haunting this town's streets,
our walks cut into neat
desperate portions of breath.

Now he's free and I stay in

and the nut cage swings
with winter at its wire

and someone else's dog barks.

Sheds

A friend opened his, dressed it
in ribbons; speeches were made.
A priest blessed it.

The public queued to get in,
surprised to find nothing inside
but the soul of a shed, a man.

*

The one I inherited fell apart.
Others might have knocked it down.
Too many ghosts to hurt

I watched it decompose –
kennel, bird's nest (flown)
sanctuary for the breeze ....

*

The village halls of Wales squat
and let the rain do its worst,
are sometimes mistaken for toilets.

*

An arch, two pews, a man,
a boy, a flask's chalice –
the putty-wafer communion.

Doorsteps crumble in the mouth.
When the elder smiles
tar burns between his teeth.

★

Ah, the ubiquitous writing shed,
sky-blue, the sun on its crest,
its wings lined with lead,

where the raging heart's affairs
were secretly confessed,
hoping someone might hear.

Boys

I need them, to muscle in on this silence,
to measure the softening tissue in my arms
when I carry them up to their beds,
when the old house creaks like a galleon
after a storm.

Set adrift on their dreams
their faces turn soft again.
So that one kiss carries the weight
of all we try to make light of.

Twelve

I was twelve when I murdered for silence.
The senile hero from number nine
trained me to shoot straight.

Silence played a deeper tune
than my father's violin,
its bullets swifter and cleaner
than any note his dusty bow could fire.

So I shot this thrush in its hedge,
allowing it one last song –
the lullaby my mother sang,
my sister's piccolo in flight ...

before silencing it
and something else, forever.

I watched it fall through its cage,
the instinct to sing
still alive in its wings

then listened again.

        A sea wind
bowed the field of reeds beyond.

Llangorse

When the lake froze
Major Raikes walked on it,
boys threw stones on it,
Prosser prayed on it,
Jean Drew painted it ...

and you and I,
after they'd all fallen through
the night's long crack,
just stared at it,
listened to moonlight creak.

Our boat, set in its grip,
would have done for a bed
but, older than our years,
we knew, or thought we did,
that the moon on the lake was enough.

Talking Ghosts

My father's talking ghosts, and poltergeists.
When he gesticulates his wedding ring
flies off.

                The blood drains from his face
into his half-ironed shirt.

                        He's dressed
the bony music stand with one of her songs,
shaded the *Steinway's* leg from the window's glare.

Diminished to their labels, three bars
of *Cussons Imperial Leather* swim in the sink.

Everything in the bungalow has shrunk

except for the silence, and the goldfish
who mime the same aria, hour by hour
and grow in exact proportion to their tank.

He's on to reincarnation now, and mediums
whose fishbowls teem with lies.

                             Only the sun
haunts, drifting across the mantelpiece,
the variations of her smile,

finding his ring on the floor again.

Maeshendre

A rush of small soles on the pavement
passes and is gone.
A bustle of wings takes off.

A Window on the Sea

That split-second, primeval glance.
Forgive me for even recording it
but, stuck to an office ceiling's
polystyrene tile, all year,
a strand of tinsel reminds me that
beyond the telescopic view
where concrete gives way to sky
there has to be sea.

My screen-saver's Cardigan Bay.
I type then stare at cumuli,
print them out in waves.
Perhaps I am the tide.
My chest rises and falls.
There's salt on my breath.
Wind your way down to me.
Pitch your psychedelic towel
and let me stroke your feet.
Drift out to sleep
in that weightless hour
between one and two
when chief executives dream.

Already I'm half way up the beach,
setting pools in the dips of you,
exploring every cove of you
where concrete gives way to sky
and fixed grins relax in heaps.

No more whip-rounds, innuendoes,
paper knives in the back ....
No more waiting twelve months
for the tinsel in your hair.
Just listen to that shell on your desk
calling you to the sea.

Marine Terrace

for Julia Bentham

Here's anywhere now, another life.
It hangs by the hinges of wings

or swims in the sea's terraces
beneath the surface of our days.

Inside *The Cabin*, a new breath blows
the surf from the cappuccinos

and where the stonemason's was
Westcoast Tattoo's moved in.

So we grieve them by this rose
on a thigh, this buttock's butterfly,

our town's unfashionable dead.

★

Sometimes, when it's calm enough
to row out into the bay and drift

we can hear the wreck of a *Bechstein* –
Miss Puw, LRCM

playing duets again, with her tail
or teaching Scott Joplin to those

whose fingers slipped between the scales.

Her doorbell holds its pitch then sinks
like a wish into the vestibule.

Behind frayed nets, watching us still,
a shoal of startled eyes.

As Close as it Gets

Perhaps if they made love, once
in a cheap hotel
where the shower's broken
and the dead fly on the window sill
won't tell, once
then it would be enough.

They meet in the late August rain.
There's a place off the Rue de Lape
with a mannequin on Reception
and no light in the stairwell.
By the time they reach the room
he's held her that close
it's almost as close as it gets,
closer than wet hair.

Above the bed a boy and girl
stroll through a fishing village
down to a biblical sunset.

The overhead fan stops.
A damp summer's intimacies
begin to turn stale.

A last kiss drops
and there's nothing left to give
and this, surely, perhaps,
is all they came here for

or perhaps they want more –

to follow the boy and the girl
all the way down to the shore.

Nocturne

Cloudless day,
Night, and a cloudless day; ...
    Robert Graves – 'Counting The Beats'

White masts, metronomes
on the night's high tide,
keep us in time

our page turner's love.
They tock and chime
as we count the waves.

Mesmerized, we slip
between the staves,
lip to lip –

the land and the sea,
making it up,
the same symphony

from the first note
that left this quay
to the last coda

until there's only your ring
(and the lines we cast)
its chime on the railing

to the bells on the masts

now answering

from *Ingrid's Husband* (2007)

Three Trees

for J, J & I

I planted three trees, for privacy
and for feeling near to the soil.
Three ferns, two a fairer shade
of green, the middle one a clone
of my father's dark spire.
(One Spring, he swapped his violin
for a spade).

     I planted three trees.
Leisurely climbers, I loved them,
suddenly taller when I turned
to look at them again.
Perhaps I planted them too close.
The wind blows in from the sea
and they seem to conspire
against me.

     I planted three trees.
It snows. Sand hurries
through the kitchen's hourglass.
I am nearer the soil
than ever I intended to be.
Above me

     three, fern-haired men
point to the cold stars,
all is silence, but for a spade
played out of key.

The Snow Dome

First sun, then snow... my father floats up the lane
in white jeans, a white rose in his claw.
He cuts a Lear-like figure, drifting alone
through the sun and snow.

Wherever your mother goes, I follow
he mutters, brushing the icing from her stone,
its doorstep to a colder house. It snows

and shines about the ornamental scene.
We can't see for the petals of the rose.
He says she kissed his bald head in the lane,
first with sun, then snow.

Duets

The night my mother died I followed
my father's car into the night.

The lights on that loneliest of roads
like an order of monks, heads bowed,
lit only their drizzled habits.

Their prayers fizzled out into darkness,
led nowhere except to her silence,
the bungalow where we shared a room,

my father and I, who had not spoken
for ten years, let alone sung
a duet together, of howls

in identical pyjamas, in twin beds.

★

My father composes himself
at the Steinway, presses *PLAY*

on the tape machine
and waits for her first note ...

(Handel's *V'adoro, pupille*
which, by good fortune

she sang unaccompanied
in F Major, for visitors,

one bright afternoon
in 1974.)

Gestures

I could, of course,
walk to your house
and die on its step.

Warm from your bed,
mistaking my rattling
teeth for the milk

you'd open the door
in pink slippers
and find me lying there

with one eye open.

★

I spy ... the last star
to disappear
through a giant curler in your hair.

★

In your absence
which is the rest of my life
and unlike Archimedes

who calculated the earth's mass
in grains of sand

I will devote my sentence
to counting the minutes
as they fall

through the hourglass of your days.

★

The cat idles on my chest.
I hold your letter up to the sky.

How to decipher
your feline *y*'s, crucified *t*'s
open-topped *a*'s and *o*'s?

The cloudy watermark
becomes a woman's face.

★

I want you close before I go.
I want you in the fire's glow
then outside in the graveyard's dirt.

I want you where the tide is low
and the sea's lips barely part
for breath to say "I told you so."

I want you close before I go.

★

I've made you my password.
Your name lets me in each day,
your name and your age.

Absurd, how these plastic keys
diminish you, stay silent
when your name is played

and how easily, without knowing,
you let me in each day.

★

Once I whispered in your ear
in the shrubbery of a summer.
Remember?

I even bought you a ring.
That was something.
Can you hear me singing

at the kiss-gate still,
at the sea wall?
Did we meet at all?

*

Here's something cold for you –
the intelligence of water.
(I should like to see you shiver.)

Lay down in its equation.
It will soon work you out,
intricately at first, then harder

lifting your back from the bed
so you're half-fish, half-woman.

Years after you've surfaced
shivering, golden, I'll be here,
student of the river

the cold pool where you lay.

*

It must have happened years ago,
this light between us, this hurt.
I want you close before I go.

*

In the fire's glow,
in the graveyard's dirt,
where the tide is low ...

★

Who will console this room
now that you've come and gone?

The wind in the chimney?
The smouldering grate?

The last star
in its universe burns

then disappears.

October

The sun lurched back and fore
all the way down to the shore.

Facing out the rain and sea
the doll's house pastels seemed to say

Once you were fair, now you are grey
while we have stayed this way.

Untied, the wrong dog flew
after another dog's shadow.

Come back, damn you! he called,
feeling the wind's chill.

The Viewing

In the tiled hall
her horned bust of Venus
keeps its style

for all the lovers' beads
about its smile.

*

Here's her portrait.
I've seen its double
in those sixties thrillers,
sandy paperbacks she's kept
in the loo, for their titles:

The Snow Was Black
by Georges Simenon;
Léo Malet's *Micmac Moche
au Boul' Mich'*; Ed McBain's
Lady, Lady, I Did It!

Or, *Walk Softly, Witch*
by Carter Brown
whose smitten private eye,
drawn to its *femme fatale's*
"magnetic" legs,

compares himself to
an iron filing.

*

I suspect her life
had known such heights
as the model
in the Blunenfeld poster
on her bedroom wall,
who might

        or might not
let go of the Eiffel Tower,
who is poised
between flight and fall,
her dress an opened fan.

I'll quit tomorrow
her ashtray says.

★

A fridge magnet's
History of Art –
from da Vinci to Warhol,
nine doodled faces,
Van Gogh's without an ear,
Dali's a squeezed balloon –
lies in the dog's bowl.

Did she burn her lip
on this Twin Towers cup?

★

Outside, her bicycle
leans, tilted, just so.

Cobwebs tie it to the tree
in case a thief should call.

Between Two Bridges

See, now they vanish,
The faces and places, with the self which, as it could, loved them,
To become renewed, transfigured, in another pattern.

T.S. Eliot – 'Little Gidding'

8pm

Wind scales the river in its mud.
It squirms and pirouettes to the tide's score –
dance of a reptile, forging its cast in silt.

Here comes a friendly stray, with marble eyes.
And here, someone's ditched a fridge. Boats
ghost-boats, Anon's boarded-up work

wait beyond plank and oil drum jetties
for names to be painted back: *Angela* ...
Dragonfly ... *Pride of Newport* ... *Norma's Ark* ...

I look for her name. (It brought me here
from clearer water, twenty years upstream.)
A swan drifts down to a castle's ruin.

A train crosses. On board's my teenage ghost.
"Tonight," he mimes, "I'll walk these streets with you.
I'll break my journey here. We'll walk all night

then one of us will stay and one take flight."

Redundant steel poles form a queue.
Their heads sprout dead sprigs, buds
whose clenched fists shake at the blue sky,

its sails drifting, too easily, out to sea.

11pm

I meet him inside a symmetrical park,
where Edwardians, in ghostly whites
swing massive pendulums

and the moon rolls through football goals.

I meet him where they can't touch us –
the bridge limpers, the black eyes,
the vet bills for three-legged dogs,

the piss emporiums, the furnaces,
the palest faces to miss
the last train home.

I meet him inside a symmetrical park.
We touch fingers, touch trees,
kick through shallow leaves

through Hornbeam, Sallow Willow,
Maidenhair, Flowering Ash ...

The smoky heads on glass pillows,
the limpers from east to west
in time for the last bus

they can't touch us.

2am

I follow his stagger up Stow Hill.
Taxi lights transfigure him,
draped in plastic road signs:

chevrons, white arrows
on blue shields – King Cone.

The wind beats its head on stone,
on glass, on Linda Barker's smile.

Perhaps he has walked from hell
and perhaps I am dreaming him
but I follow him, past lock-ups

where a hell's angel's dream,
in pieces, is shown the light.

I follow him over the motorway.

Tracks, pylons, scrapyards ...
the town's raw nerves
twinkle, a child's dream

lulled in the moon's headlamp.

I follow him under a railway bridge,
its thin, wire whine of breaks
or is it the wind's harmonica?

Between two bridges I follow him

past a wave sculpted in steel,
a boat they found inside the mud
and thought an ark to save the port ...

The same current underfoot
drags us on. I can't keep up.

I catch the breath of those who drowned
to keep afloat this listing town,
the steel hull of it.

Only the wind raises them
and a few words perhaps, a name

cut in marble or wood.
(I am not too drunk to salute them.)

The bank runs out. He sheds his cape.
A smudged lamp erases him.

The cradle under the big bridge
ferries its souls back and fore ...

The river shuffles on to the sea.

5am

The river's nightshift nears its end, slips through an arch of daylight.
Cranes, their loads still, have caught nothing but stars all night.

The first train. His face in mine and, mirrored, a half-raised hand.
He should smile. Soon he'll be walking greener banks with his friends,
setting nightlines, building fires, though I shan't envy him

except when he's drinking it dry and, walking in this later time,
I notice the river, barely a slough of itself in the cracked mud –
as if the moon had taken a long straw to the years and sucked.

He pulls away. The wind puts its lips to an arcade.
A seagull on a barber's pole waits to open its blades.

8am

Wind scales the river in its mud.
It squirms and pirouettes to the tide's score –
dance of a reptile, forging its cast in silt.

Here comes the stray with marble eyes.
He seems to belong here. I watch him
chase and bark the river on its way.

And here, someone's ditched a red armchair.
Prifardd of mud, I lounge in it.
A train crosses. A swan sails near.

Downstream, the cradle ferries its load
back and fore, back and fore ...
as town and river rise from their beds.

Like parts of a clock the small boats
and their jetties rise. I look for her name,
the woman who brought me here. If I wait

I might drift, between two bridges, in my chair
like *Angela ... Dragonfly ... Pride of Newport ...
Norma's Ark ...* I might find her.

*Note. "Prifardd": tr. "Chief Bard" – upon whom a
chair is bestowed at eisteddfodau.*

Six Men in Search of a Car

They have left their desks in mid sentence,
come out into the early rush hour
to push a car that isn't there.

They have turned a corner, in unison,
a makeshift pack, crew, squadron
because this is what men do well

on a field, at sea, in the air ....

But there is nothing to put muscle into,
no war, no coalface

only this space, and redundancy
in the faces of six men

as if the lift they descended in
had suddenly jolted between floors.
Where's the bloody car?

Steel melts in their arms. They turn

and lean towards a light breeze,
to disparate spaces in offices
filled with women's voices.

Three Women Running for a Bus

Not a race but three women running
after their shadows, away from the sun
along a city pavement – my wife
my mother, my daughter – at 9am.
I'm on the top deck, waving at them.
It is as if the road were a treadmill,
a case of running and standing still
but my daughter's a metre in front
and my gasping mother has lost
a peach from her bag, it rolls
into the path of a cyclist.
My wife cries *Wait! Halt! Stop!*
with a traffic policewoman's arm
and I'm calling back like a fish
miming its life's soliloquy

but they can't hear for the glass
which will rain onto their heads.
The driver pulls away from the kerb.
Just look at their desperate faces,
like a red bus was all they had loved.

Ingrid's Husband

The roadside leaves leapt out
as if to flag me down.

I stopped for some razor-blades.
The shop assistant asked
Are you Ingrid's husband?

No. But afterwards,
all the dwindling miles,
I wondered what she was like,

Ingrid, what soap she used,
if her hair was the colour
of these crazy leaves

and if she was mad or sane
or some shade in between.

Perhaps if we met
I'd grow to love her name.

I have seen leaves migrate
to parallel lives –

blown through an underpass
from the eastern side
of a motorway to the west.

Perhaps I should have answered *Yes*.

The Skylight

Somewhere our belonging particles
Believe in us. If we could only find them.
   W.S. Graham – 'Implements in Their Places'

It's summer outside this winter house
with its fire in every room.
Two seagulls cross the skylight.
Yesterday it was snow-dust
they picked through, instead of sand
and the waves chose not to break.

The same light, in the long break
of '69, visited this house.
We'd had our swim and the sand
stuck to us. We sat in this room,
said nothing, watched the dust
drift on its current of light,
had little in common but that light
which would see fit to break
throughout our lives, stirring old dust.

Each wave of sunlight then, in this house,
carries the two of us in that room,
carries our dust, our grains of sand.

                    ★

Shaping a fish out of sand
you made it a race against the light,
the sea, the crowds... there was no room.
Build and break, build and break ...
I followed you up to the house.
Our wet prints dissolved to dust
in the narrow lane.

Here, moondust.
I touched your palm, the dusty sand
felt precious.

Back inside the house
we played cards under the skylight,
I waited for the silence to break.

★

I have waited in so many rooms,
particles of this spinning room.
I have lived inside the dust
of wanting you, afraid to break
like the fish you shaped out of sand.

★

Two seagulls cross the skylight.
It's summer outside our winter house.
There is room for a ghost or two on the sand.

★

That's me, that's you ... dust in the sunlight.
We swim and break and drift about this house.

The White Balloon

In a dark arcade
there is only this white balloon

and the echoes of my steps
trying to keep up with it

always a metre ahead
on its current of air.

A square of light grows
in the distance.

I break into a run.
The balloon picks up its pace

swerves off course
when I try to kick it.

Once I was a child
on a wide beach

chasing a big ball
the wind had stolen.

Breathless now,
in a dark arcade

my heart echoes after
a white balloon.

The Black Guitar

Clearing out ten years from a wardrobe
I opened its lid and saw *Joe*
written twice in its dust, in a child's hand,
then a squiggled seagull or two.

                            Joe, Joe
a man's tears are worth nothing,
but a child's name in the dust, or in the sand
of a darkening beach, that's a life's work.

I touched two strings, to hear how much
two lives can slip out of tune

                         then I left it,
brought down the night on it, for fear, Joe
of hearing your unbroken voice, or the sea
if I played it.

Five Notes from St Rémy

I

Is it the only note the wind knows –
this orange beachball on a pool?
It makes no sound, no tune.
Inside, a Satie nocturne
waits, forever, on the piano.

II

Can you hear?
Three fields away, someone
is learning the musical saw
in A. Listen ...
Is it the only note they know?

III

A hammock creaks from a lime.
Francoise wears it like a toga,
trails an arm in leafy shallows.
Is it the only note she knows?
I decorate her hair with a rose.

IV

A bookish dog, disturbed
by lavender in the key of A
(is it?) lifts up his head
from Dali's *Journal d'un Genie*
as if, as if to say

V

Borne across the sky
on a white tray a cicada
ends its *Fugue for Beard and Saw*
with the only note it knows –
a drop, before a downpour.

Summer Reading

Bernard Spencer and Disneyland don't mix
but a book entitled *With Luck Lasting*'s a must
to get me through the week.

                Titania,
our cloned chalet, stinks. Radios blare:
a World Service tribute to 'The King',
Prague and Dresden, bailing out their floods,
the two missing girls ...

                On small verandas,
to keep off the sun, the red, white and yellow
Miko flower turns on its stalk.
Those obsessed with roundabouts and food
grow fat beneath it, smile

                    while too high
to see, beyond 'the nothing of the air'
a hawk tunes its dial.

The Waiting Room

An empty coatstand in a public building, in August.
Even this is draped with your absence.
The rags of a seagull's cry hang from it now.

Nothing is devoid of love.
How many years did I waste, listening out
for your voice?

              The park through a window,
swollen with leaves, smothers its coatstands well.

Thin veils of clouds, a city's prayers,
fall away to the west. For a split second
I can see your eyes.

                But if I break my gaze
the gull has slipped its hook, the sea
is a long way away.

The Stooge

The café at Orcombe Point
vanished like a magician's prop
from its stone plinth.

Laughter from the sky.

Here's where he sat,
staring, sip after sip,
easily taken in by the tide.

Applause from the strand.

Dark handkerchiefs.
An occasional white gull
shaken up to the clouds.

Lone heckler.

The radio played Acker Bilk's
Stranger on the Shore.
The waitress wore a pinafore.

Red flag, white flag ....

From east to west the sun
waved its bright wand
across his stupid face.

A curtain of rain.

Did he not hear
the sea's knuckles click
before he disappeared?

Smoke.   Music.

Leaf Man

Leaves, the sky's loose change
glance against the pane.
Look! I am rich in leaves.
I shall step out of this frame
into an October garden
and, staring into the sun,
stuff my jacket with leaves.

Secure in the currency of leaves
I shall not work again
but strut my good fortune
from season to season,
car park to museum,
Winter's "Any change?"
brushed aside with a wave.

All glances are leaves.
I am rich in leaves.
I shall fill each room
of this gallery's mansion
with leaves, and dream
on a bed of leaves,
the next best thing to love.

Leaves, the sky's loose change.
I am rich in leaves.
Staring into the sun
my jacket brims with them.
I shall not work again
but rustle from season
to season, a man of leaves.

College Library

The book no one else took out
since stamped on 9.10.80
when the Jack Russell froze on its zebra
four stripes ahead of its zimmer
and a wave held back its confession
and a tongue hovered an inch from its cone
and the lifeboat got anchored to its wake
and a finger in the Bay View's window
accused the horizon ... is still here.

He splits it, gently, its shell
back to the light. They take a breath
as swimmers surfacing might.
Their fingertips drift, collide
on lines once whispered by heart.
He snaps it shut again, for good.
The esplanade clock chimes twenty-five ....

Small lines appear at her eyes, which he loves.
His hair comes away in her hand when they kiss.
Someone says *Sh* – a pair of heels on wood
near where the sun falls open at their feet.

Two Violins

The estate will not be built
for another fifty years.

There is only this mist
a shuffle of wings overhead

and ... listen

                    two violins

trying to find each other.

Shed

It was either a mountain or this shed in the rain.
Someone has felted its roof and I'm dry.
Dead spiders hang against the pane,
their legs the broken spokes
of abandoned umbrellas. A web shakes
as heavy thunder rolls down the valley.

I have known worse waiting rooms,
in hospitals, prisons, railway stations ...
A sense of travelling inside the rain,
sustained by flying leaves and the drum
of a thousand fingers, keeps me here.

Two spiders survive. One has crossed
the misted pane to reach the other.

I have known worse places to be lost.

Sold

Others want this house and soon
we must either leave or stay.
Is it the house or love
we are moving out of?
Perhaps we cannot say

but it hurts, all afternoon
our marriage has moved inside me –
the boys, the prints on the stairs,
the broken-down cars, the holidays
in heaven and hell, long Saturdays
in market towns, mad neighbours .

I pick you a pear from the tree
but you have disappeared again
into that silence you inhabit,
your second home, where a whisper
might fall heavily to the floor –
an incendiary, pear-shaped
and loaded with pain.

Shall we stay or leave then, love?
It's only the years moving inside us
and everything hurts in autumn.
Where shall we put them,
the years, in our new house?
the years we are moving out of?

New Poems

The Brittle Sea

Dear Ghost, this lunch hour
I am all glass for you,
office block become man.
I lie down in pieces, in Bute Park
and wink back at the sun.

You are the same white cloud
in each of my thousand panes.
You are only a cloud-ride away.

The city's mechanical tide
builds and rebuilds relentlessly.
Dust and din. It will not rest.
Pity its rocks – Bute,
Bevan, Batchelor ...
Cranes play chess with them.

And though I would settle for
the accidental brush
of your hand on a shop door
right now I would sooner hold you
inside the sea's architecture

taste the salt on your lips
my glass palm on your shoulder
your blue eyes peering into me ...
This longing, dear Ghost
builds and rebuilds inside me.

Where are you? I must get back
to my desk in the sky.

A builder drops his hammer
as Madame Vanborough,
Howells' milliner,
sweeps down Morgan Arcade.

The city's souls are restless.
Is there time to catch your cloud
before it vanishes?

Grey suits in hard hats
swarm the Hayes, their plan
(which failed with pigeons
and God and the sea)
to redevelop the sky.

They study the blueprint,
shield their eyes

and I wonder, dear Ghost,
in the absence of a cloud,
if a glass man might fly.

The Drunk and The Night Runner

This bench, between the sea
and the castle, tell me,
what colour did they choose
for the serpents' hundredth coat?
I only remember sky blue.

As you run past, by moonlight
I raise my head, disturbed
by the rhythm of your feet
against the rhythm of the tide.
It is the rhythm of my heart.

I raise an arm, to wave
only to wave, my love.
And perhaps you wave too,
wave back, as you run past.

Dodging the Waves

The gap between the railings was thirty-five years.
The boy's ghost held on as the high tide raged
and the girl beside him laughed when she too got drenched.
"Who turned all the fairy lights blue?" "Who cares?"

The sea slid back down its pebbly stairs.
"Here comes a big one. Don't let go!" "Never!
I'll never let go!"

              And both held on to the white bar
before both let go, their laughter caught inside the wave.

Vilnius Umbrellas

From the dry side of a window watch them glide,
such ecstasies as umbrellas hide.

Lovers beneath them were never this close, the lonely
never so alone. An unborn child rides slowly
sheltered twice over.

Under a broken pink one
a tall black coat, under a leopard-skin one
a leopard-skin woman!

Here's cupola turned whirligig.
Wet through, its owner dances – somewhere between a jig
and Gene Kelly.

Already you love this city,
its collapsible domes, its tears and its treaties
writ in glass.

Janina

Deep in your Soviet sleeping block
the corridors last forever,
doors wail on their hinges
and close like shots in a tunnel.

Do not be sad, Janina,
at the crack in your cell's mirror,
at the creature in your eye.
All of our unoiled hearts
are echoing inside
and the corridors of love have no end.

Put on your pearl necklace
and head for the northern marshes.
Someone will take you there, I am sure.
And smile, as you wait,
at how quietly
the leaves escape their hinges

to fall where they will
or where the wind dictates.

Penllain

In love with an absence
I have wasted my days
believing in this house.

Your limpet ghost clings
to the walls of its rock.
Each night another wave

breaks over you, but you cling
like Gwyneth Blue's painting
and this dust is yours

this sofa where a girl
hugged her knees
and sucked her bony thumb.

Here's where Geta sat,
her old age making profound
the simplest act.

This room's her rockpool still.

Hauling herself up
truth is, she fairly darts
about her element.

There!
She gives the Bush t.v. a slap.

Where did she flit to then,
her shadow? To what switch,
handle, fabric, utensil?

Ah, she was only pouring tea.
Does china rattle under water?
Does time dart or shuffle?

I'll tilt the blinds
so the sun slides off you.
Forgive me, I have to

get the angle, so you are
always Brown Helen.

I've let in a schoolyard's cries
and birdsong
but louder than these

what the sun says to *Penllain*,
what *Penllain* replies –

Geta? Is that you?
Gwyneth Blue?

Let me read you
The Song of Solomon
from Enoch's bible.

Its dark, spineless fossil
lies buried deep on the sill.

Enoch, who begat Geta
who begat Gwyneth Blue
who begat Brown Helen ...

Do you mind, Enoch?
It's a bit, you know
ewn but here we go –

"Agorais i'm hanwylyd;
ond fy anwylyd a giliasai,
ac a aethai ymaith ..."

The megalithic clock translates.

Some brass in the grate,
the doll's head of a broken brush ...
Few childhood barnacles remain.

Whose footprints are these
on the sandy floor's mosaic?

They raced through my castle
without disturbing a grain.

Your designer table's
window on a wooden frame
is moored where the piano was.

I am trying to play it now
while drowning in glass.

Dear Brown Helen,
I have wasted my days
believing in a house!

Don't laugh. Oh go on then.
How nonchalantly
your ghost haunts me.

Who were we?
Come back to this sofa
and hug your knees

and suck your bony thumb
and read me
The Song of Solomon.

I'll tilt the blinds
so the sun's wave slides off you.

I am a man
come back to this house.

Come back my limpet ghost.

Note. st. 19 – ewn – tr. bold, daring
st.20 – tr. "I opened for my lover / but my lover had left; /
he was gone." (Song of Solomon - Chp. 5 v.6)

Catrin Sands

Catrin Sands, are you still there?
I dreamt about you last night.
You think it's all Brown Helen but it's you
who were pale and thin last night.
And your eyes were brown instead of blue
Catrin Sands, if you're still there.

The sea was a long way below
the wooden room I found you inside,
pale and thin, in a white blouse.
You looked at me with your new eyes
like you never did as a child.
The sea was a long way below.

There was something you needed to say,
my ear to your lips as you tried
but the sea, forty years below,
drowned all I wanted to know.
So I held you close, in case we had died
with something you needed to say.

Catrin Sands, are you still there?
I dreamt about you last night.
You think it's all Brown Helen but it's you
who were pale and thin last night.
And your eyes were brown instead of blue
Catrin Sands, if you're still there.

Nightingale Ann

Ann Walters, forgive me
for troubling your silence.

It is not the minim's echo
nor the quaver's arrow
but the spaces between the notes
I am trying to hear.

Did you clear your throat then?
Is that what I almost heard?

An intake of breath.
Was it mine or yours?

The rustle of a concert gown.

You raise an eyebrow
and Keats's nightingale takes flight.
Or was it Edward Thomas's unknown bird?

Ann, it's been eight years.
Forgive my untrained ear.

It is not the minim's echo
nor the quaver's arrow
but the spaces between the notes
I am trying to hear.

Prydwen Jane

A picnic in Wiltshire sees you
limp off "for a ciggy, dear."

You catch your breath on a gate.
"I'm at death's door, dear!"

(That or you'll be the final
visitor to leave.)

On a slope beyond you
well-heeled children pull
and feel the pull of the sky.

You raise your walking stick,
make a glockenspiel of the gate.

Is that *God Save the Queen*
or *O Na Byddain Haf o Hyd?*

The stick's a cricket bat now.
"Ninety not out!"

Smell the air, Prydwen!
And let me inhale
some of it with you.

And give me your hand.

I must keep you from taking off
like the kite woman
in Chagall's *Promenade.*

I must keep you
from the pull of the sky.

Edith's Transistor Radio

Went with her from room to room
tuned to the Third Programme

a small cathedral beside her chair
on Sunday evenings, organ and choir

competing with sanctimonious prayer
but mostly it was an orchestra

she had trapped in its blue case,
hostages to her loneliness. Her face

when once I tried to release them
across the dial to Hilversum.

They were doomed to the mid century,
their suits, frocks and hair turned grey

with the dust of her boredom
like a hundred Miss Havershams.

But she loved her Elgar, Brahms,
Beethoven … her Vaughan Williams

and, more than Verdi, it was Mozart
she adored – *The Magic Flute*,

called me her little Papageno.
I heard an almost famous soprano

plead for her freedom one afternoon.
The sunlit curtains were drawn.

Branches barred the window pane.
Outside, the birds were calling for rain.

Steel

(i) 10

Turn like a key
in the game's lock
and open the score
with a kick –
open a door in the air
onto blue sky.

I dreamt I opened a door
in the sky
and half the world cheered.
I dreamt I surfaced
into a roar.
No sky was like this before.

Dart like a hare
through a hedge at dusk
and open the score
with a try –
open a door
in the earth.

I dreamt I opened a door
in the earth
and rose into light
out of an underworld
where, for years,
I carried their ghosts on my back.

Flash like a link
in a steel chain
like the sun on the sea
or a wave
in the industry
of a rising tide.

I dreamt I surfaced
into a roar.
The seagulls
shrill as whistles
were red and white.
I dreamt my ghosts had taken flight.

(ii) 15

Still, but less often
there is time to look up
and catch an idea as it falls.

There is time to save
or fumble a planet,
to catch its dewy head

and nurse it
close to your chest,
to your heart.

A theatre's eyes
are upon you and still
there is this moment

as time's egg
spins on its axis,
this dazzling light

between birth and death,
this sharp intake of breath.

(iii) Steel

I felled a tree
with my bare hands.
I ran through a forest.
I sifted its branches for gold.
No border guard could hold me.

Soon, my country
you will be rich.

Your rivers run through my veins.
Your tides and mountains
swell in my chest.
Your birds of prey
are my arms and legs in flight.
I have fifteen hearts.

Inside this steel frame
the wheels of your valleys
turn again, spin
and catch the sun.

I am steel in flight,
unstoppable –
a dragon with fifteen hearts.

Soon, my country ...

Nothing can stop me now.

Clock

To keep us in time I've bought this clock
that ticks and strikes in its own time.
I think it is several, pieced-together clocks
but no matter, it chimes
on its almost hour and that will do.

You should hear it tick without you.
Like a rocking-horse wild for its ghost.
I rest a palm against my chest
and think my heart might chime
as the long hand nears midnight.

Now.   Listen.   For you.   Twelve times ...

and now the wild horse again, into the night.

The Lichen Gatherer

Make sure the doors to this wood are locked.
Look, here's some moss, or lichen is it,
for you. It's wet but it'll soon dry out
like this burnt sienna mud, pocked
and stippled with those who passed through us.

The ghosts of old loves can't find us here.
The rafters leak a little with sky
and, yes, there are too many doors to check
but I think we will be safe here for a while
inside our tangled metaphor.

                  So smile,
and kiss me, before this moss or lichen dries.

Song

When you were nine, and hurt
I had a room like this, a garret.
I had five years' worth of songs
and a window that shook with the sea.
I had everything.
Between the glass and the shore
there were similar trees
confused by the wind.
And the same fine rain
made cuts in the small panes,
the nine portions of light
that were my days and nights.

How distant it seems now,
that time when I had everything
and nothing, when you were nine
and hurt, and, without knowing it,
I sang you this song.

The Forty-year-old Cocktail Dress

That shadow on Prof. Gowan's lawn, I know it's you
drifting about the agbadas and saris.
The sixties fit you perfectly.

You wave to me through bars between the staves.
You've blown my cover. *Shush.*
Blow me a kiss then.

Blow me a kiss or I'll tell, I'll make you climb
that balcony, confess MacNeice's
Prayer Before Birth.

The sun pinks out across the bay, on its slide.
A kiss? It's still allowed, to blush
on Planet Earth.

Or let me touch the soft blades on your arm.
Or let's play catch, adagio
across the unborn years.

A cork is launched into space.

My mother calls me in.

*

The curtains' blue fish darken.
They are darkening, my love.
How can a boy sleep when

inside the drowned persiflage
of Prof. Gowan's soirée
another glass kisses yours

or when, inside the darkest of tides
I can still hear your laugh?

The Prayer Room

Your prayers could live in this room.
The clock would keep them in time.
It's late. There is lamplight
and moonlight, and two skylights.

Your eyes looked down on me
earlier. I could see the sea
when I tilted a pane and looked out.
Perhaps you heard me shout.
It is only three hundred miles.
I have heard men in gaols
call from cells to their wives
across busy roads, call to their loves.

If you came here now, and prayed
and taught me to pray ...
If you came here once
to hear the clock, the silence,
I might close my eyes on myself
and simply forget myself
in your voice.

                    Waves of prayers
break over me, my wasted years.
See how the tide takes me out
into darkness. But for this moonlight
I've disappeared. Who are we
but ghosts on the night's sea?

Your prayers could live inside me.
Say a prayer now, for company
and it may reach this lonely room.
I'll open a skylight in time
to let you in.

The Distance of Rooms

In the coldest meeting room, a smile
is sometimes enough and, though still,
the floor might secretly have wheels.

Hold onto your chair. Here we go
through tunnel after tunnel – a slide-show
of castles and bloodlit winter fields.

See how the ice lies, like knives,
like trayfuls of surgical knives –
the instruments that kill and heal.

And here is that brassy river, your hair
when 'Folk in The Foyer'
made you place a finger in each ear.

This room then, racing, and us still here.
And all that turns inside us is concealed.

From 'The History of The Café Bar.'

after Eugenijus Alisanka

My friends grow older.
Homer, half-cut, senile
tells the same tale
from his Soviet naval days,
how some radioactive cargo
nearly triggered off a war
in the Black Sea. "Cherchez la femme"
he mutters, "Cherchez la femme."

Dante trembles in a corner.
Dead and living blur
through his empty spyglass.
His ashtray is a funeral pyre.

If this is Alzheimer's,
dancing with St Vitas
between the tables,
waltzing with Helen
whose name I've forgotten,
whose bones will be the ashes
of all my wishes.
If this is Alzheimer's ...

Blind Odysseus starts a scuffle.
Those who are still here
curse, carry their visions of Hell
into the afternoon glare.

Sand

It is the same for me – a winter beach
and kissing the heartbeat in your wrist ...
but we are not real.

                             We are fine sand
and the congregation of fine sand
builds yet more dunes for the lost.

We are lost. Listen. The sea's ache
in a shell is our music. Hush.
Listen. But know it will diminish.

Arcades

Already you're gone, fixing your eyes
on a road's darkening arcade.

What song do you sing as the light fades?

The music shop you work in has closed
but I have to believe it is not too late.

Is it your eyes or your laugh I miss most?

I'd buy you those boots or that bracelet
your mother wore, or an amber ring

to prove it is not too late to sing,
to prove we are more than worn out ghosts.

Dream in arcades, love. Dream in arcades.

Violin Tide

And this is the sea, of course
scrawling by moonlight in its room,
not quite getting the line right
where it meets the shore.

The earliest hours still find me
thinking of you; somnolent tides
rise towards daylight.
Perhaps you have drowned in me.

A table lamp shines the grain
of an old violin in the grate
and down the slope from your dreams
the bay similarly shines.

Perhaps you are not so far away
from the moon in the violin
and the clock I should wind, to hear
the workings of the bay.

At least in your dreams
see how I can not get this line
to make sense of the sand,
and how I am running out of time

and how easily the night and the day
exchange places, the land and the sea.

Nine Boys Hid

The Bentham boys are waking up as men
with goatees and soft chandeliers
of hair masking the sleep in their eyes.
Bed-springs creak, adjust to their weight.
The quiet music room keeps time, looks out
to the white garden where they played, its tree
clutching at sky. And where the snow lies
nine boys hid, nine men found them.

Nine six-footers, they disappear
at intervals, to colonise the poles
but always return to Catford S.E.6,
to shared rooms emerging from the dark
like dusty negatives held up to the light.
Perhaps their mother's voice brings them back.
In the key of fried bacon it climbs the stairs –
some aria that nursed their smaller souls.

Beyond the garden, the fall of a train's brakes
is like an aircraft landing, a deepening yawn.
Arms stretch. A pillow frames a face.
Out of the snow where nine boys hid, they surface,
nine men, one by one, by one, by one ...

Flames

It was chance that she'd sat down
in a crowded churchyard by the grave
of an old boyfriend who died young.
And that her heart had just broken again.

It was like he'd called her over
to say, "There, there; never mind.
Ours was an innocent love."

She put some wild flowers against his stone
then came back after a windy night
to check they had survived.
And they had.

Like small flames in a dark hearth
they danced for no one else but her.

Moonlight

for Clare Bentham

Dark movements gather outside the French windows.
Clare, will you play me the *Moonlight Sonata?*
Piano stool: high enough. Pedals: on tiptoes.
Play now. *Adagio sostenuto.*

Ferns in the pane are like crazy conductors,
hair blown wild in the moonlight, dark figures.
Play on, my innocent, time is this blue room.
Small hands are turning the tides of the moon.

Over the waves of my youth a soprano,
over the chords of this very same piano
sailed her big voice, day and night. I ignored it,
fingers in ears while others adored it.

Sometimes I stand on a shoreline and listen.
Thinking I hear her I scan the horizon.
Clare, she has followed you here, by the moon's sail.
Small hands are washing themselves in old scales.

Dark figures mass at the window. Ignore them.
Play on, my innocent, time is this blue room.
Piano stool: high enough. Pedals: on tiptoes.
Play now. *Adagio sostenuto.*

Goble Montage

i.m. Anthony Goble

Pigeon to cockerel, pigeon to cockerel ...
Are you reading me?
Over.

You are dear to us down here
as moonlight on slate

and we need to know if, in heaven
there are beards longer
or colours brighter than yours.

Does God wear Harris tweed?
Or practise the musical saw?
Or keep a policeman's helmet
in his hall, just in case?

Pigeon word to cockerel colour:

Does the winged traffic stop
to let you cross?

Do children point
and call you Christmas
in the sun, or Rainbow Man?

Do they let you paint the red red roses red?
Or eat a burnt bacon baguette
with six cloves of garlic? Do they?

Do you ride an electric bike
or a tricycle of flowers?

Are there postman's elastic bands
on the clouds' flagstones
and, if you stamp on one
will these grey feathers take flight

like your hats in high winds?

Pigeon to cockerel, to rainbow man ...

I have driven through rain
to find your arc has vanished.
There is too much of you to describe.

On the morning you disappeared
all the angels you painted
wept inside your shed

the colours drained from the town.

The sky mixes its palette
from grey to blue
and I cannot see you

nor recall that poem you'd recite
with the French refrain
by someone who died alone
but smiled in your company.

Pigeon to cockerel.
Are you reading me?

Do both Dylans sing
in your new studio?
Has heaven gone digital yet?

And how go the charity shops?
Silk tie? Silk handkerchief?
Moleskins? Brogues? ...

What will you bring home today?
A book? A brass lady-bell
whose skirt rings?
A rosary perhaps?

What will you take in?
A walking stick
with a swan's head?

Such are the choices of kings.

Pigeon to cockerel.
Cockerel, come in ....

Across celestial wavelengths
I am trying to tune in.

You are dear to us down here
as a Winter canvas
set on fire by Spring.
Are you listening?

Not all the pigeon words
in the world
could tell your story.

Where shall we begin?
Where shall we begin?

With a painting, burning.

Acknowledgements

These are due to the editors of the following publications, in which some of the poems in this selection first appeared:

Agenda, Answering Back (Picador), *Beyond Bedlam* (Anvil), *Burning the Bracken* (Seren), *Druskininkai Poetic* Fall 2007, *The Forward Book of Poetry*, (1994, 2009, 2010), *The Gregory Anthology 1987-1990* (Hutchinson), *The Independent, In My Sky at Twilight* (MacMillan) *Intimate Portraits* (Seren/Glynn Vivian), *London Magazine, The Literary Review* (New Jersey), *The Malahat Review, Metre, New Welsh Review, New Writing 4 & 5* (Vintage), *The North, The Observer, Oxford Poetry, Oxygen* (Seren), *A Poet's Guide to Britain* (Penguin Classics), *Poetry 1900-2000* (Library of Wales), *Poetry Ireland Review, Poet Portraits (Seren), Poetry Review, Poetry Salzburg, Poetry Wales, Planet, PN Review, Reflecting Families* (BBC Education), *The Rialto, Thumbscrew, Twentieth Century Anglo-Welsh Poetry* (Seren), *South West Review, The Spectator, The Times Literary Supplement*.

'Between Two Bridges' was originally broadcast on S4C. A short film of the poem, directed by students from the International Film School Wales, was premiered at Manhattan's Tribeca Cinemas in 2008.

'The Breath of Sleeping Boys' was commissioned by the Hay Literature Festival, being one of several responses to the theme of 'War and Peace.'

'Steel' was commissioned for *Poetry in Motion*, a Greenbay production for BBC2.

The author is grateful to those who have supported his work over the years and especially to his editor, Amy Wack.

By the same author:

Time Pieces
Captive Audience
The Milk Thief
The Slipped Leash
The Breath of Sleeping Boys & other poems
Ingrid's Husband
The Black Guitar: Selected Poems (India)
Boy Running
The Glass Aisle
As If To Sing

Mari d'Ingrid (L'Harmattan, tr. Gérard Augustin)
Ragazzo di corsa (Kolibris, tr. Chiara De Luca)
Il corridoio di vetro (Kolibris, tr. Chiara De Luca)

The Slate Sea (Camden Trust, ed.)